THE OLD
FARMER'S ALMANAC
2025 PLANNER

Begin the new year square with every man.

–Robert B. Thomas, founder of
The Old Farmer's Almanac (1766–1846)

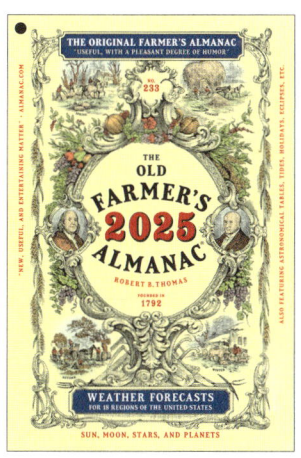

A PLANNER FILLED WITH FUN FACTS, LORE, AND MORE!

PUBLISHER: Sherin Pierce

EDITORIAL: Sarah Perreault, *writer;* Heidi Stonehill, *editor;* Catherine Boeckmann, Jack Burnett, Carol Connare, Tim Goodwin, Jennifer Keating

CREATIVE DIRECTOR: Colleen Quinnell

ART DIRECTOR: Lori Pedrick

DESIGNER: Janet Selle

PRODUCTION: David Ziarnowski, *director;* Brian Johnson, *manager;* Jennifer Freeman, Rachel Kipka

Astronomical events are given in Eastern Time.

ILLUSTRATIONS: Kristin Kest

If you find this planner, please return it to:

Name _____

Address _____

Phone (Home) _____ (Work) _____ (Cell) _____

U.S. orders: Call 800-ALMANAC (800-256-2622, option #2) or visit our
Web site at Almanac.com/Shop.
Canada orders: Visit Amazon.
For retail information, contact Stacey Korpi at 800-895-9265, ext. 160.

Printed in China

ISBN: 978-1-961793-98-9

2025 Holidays

JANUARY
1 New Year's Day
6 Epiphany
7 Orthodox Christmas (Julian)
20 Martin Luther King Jr.'s Birthday, observed
20 Inauguration Day
29 Lunar New Year (China)

FEBRUARY
1 First day of Black History Month
2 Candlemas
2 Groundhog Day
12 Abraham Lincoln's Birthday
14 Valentine's Day
15 National Flag of Canada Day
17 Presidents' Day
22 George Washington's Birthday
28 Ramadan begins at sundown

MARCH
3 Orthodox Lent begins
5 Ash Wednesday
8 International Women's Day
9 Daylight Saving Time begins at 2:00 A.M.
10 Commonwealth Day (Canada)
17 St. Patrick's Day
20 Vernal Equinox
31 César Chávez Day

APRIL
12 Passover begins at sundown
13 Palm Sunday
18 Good Friday
20 Easter
20 Orthodox Easter
21 Easter Monday
22 Earth Day
23 Holocaust Remembrance Day begins at sundown
25 National Arbor Day

MAY
1 First day of Asian American, Native Hawaiian, and Pacific Islander Heritage Month
5 Cinco de Mayo
11 Mother's Day
17 Armed Forces Day
19 Victoria Day (Canada)
22 National Maritime Day
26 Memorial Day, observed

JUNE
1 First day of Pride Month
5 World Environment Day
6 D-Day
8 Whitsunday–Pentecost
8 Orthodox Pentecost
14 Flag Day
15 Father's Day
19 Juneteenth National Independence Day
20 Summer Solstice
21 National Indigenous Peoples Day (Canada)
26 First of Muharram begins at sundown

JULY
1 Canada Day
4 Independence Day
20 International Moon Day
26 National Day of the Cowboy

AUGUST
1 Emancipation Day (Canada)
4 Civic Holiday (Canada)
19 National Aviation Day
26 Women's Equality Day

SEPTEMBER
1 Labor Day
7 Grandparents Day
11 Patriot Day
15 First day of National Hispanic/Latinx Heritage Month
17 Constitution Day
21 International Day of Peace
22 Rosh Hashanah begins at sundown
22 Autumnal Equinox
30 National Day for Truth and Reconciliation (Canada)

OCTOBER
1 Yom Kippur begins at sundown
6 Child Health Day
9 Leif Eriksson Day
12 National Farmer's Day
13 Columbus Day, observed
13 Indigenous Peoples' Day
13 Thanksgiving Day (Canada)
24 United Nations Day
31 Halloween

NOVEMBER
2 Daylight Saving Time ends at 2:00 A.M.
4 Election Day
11 Veterans Day
11 Remembrance Day (Canada)
19 Discovery of Puerto Rico Day
20 National Child Day (Canada)
27 Thanksgiving Day

DECEMBER
7 National Pearl Harbor Remembrance Day
14 Chanukah begins at sundown
15 Bill of Rights Day
17 Wright Brothers Day
21 Winter Solstice
25 Christmas Day
26 Boxing Day (Canada)
26 First day of Kwanzaa
31 New Year's Eve

2025

JANUARY
S	M	T	W	T	F	S
			1	2	3	4
5	6	7	8	9	10	11
12	13	14	15	16	17	18
19	20	21	22	23	24	25
26	27	28	29	30	31	

FEBRUARY
S	M	T	W	T	F	S
						1
2	3	4	5	6	7	8
9	10	11	12	13	14	15
16	17	18	19	20	21	22
23	24	25	26	27	28	

MARCH
S	M	T	W	T	F	S
						1
2	3	4	5	6	7	8
9	10	11	12	13	14	15
16	17	18	19	20	21	22
23	24	25	26	27	28	29
30	31					

APRIL
S	M	T	W	T	F	S
		1	2	3	4	5
6	7	8	9	10	11	12
13	14	15	16	17	18	19
20	21	22	23	24	25	26
27	28	29	30			

MAY
S	M	T	W	T	F	S
				1	2	3
4	5	6	7	8	9	10
11	12	13	14	15	16	17
18	19	20	21	22	23	24
25	26	27	28	29	30	31

JUNE
S	M	T	W	T	F	S
1	2	3	4	5	6	7
8	9	10	11	12	13	14
15	16	17	18	19	20	21
22	23	24	25	26	27	28
29	30					

JULY
S	M	T	W	T	F	S
		1	2	3	4	5
6	7	8	9	10	11	12
13	14	15	16	17	18	19
20	21	22	23	24	25	26
27	28	29	30	31		

AUGUST
S	M	T	W	T	F	S
					1	2
3	4	5	6	7	8	9
10	11	12	13	14	15	16
17	18	19	20	21	22	23
24	25	26	27	28	29	30
31						

SEPTEMBER
S	M	T	W	T	F	S
	1	2	3	4	5	6
7	8	9	10	11	12	13
14	15	16	17	18	19	20
21	22	23	24	25	26	27
28	29	30				

OCTOBER
S	M	T	W	T	F	S
			1	2	3	4
5	6	7	8	9	10	11
12	13	14	15	16	17	18
19	20	21	22	23	24	25
26	27	28	29	30	31	

NOVEMBER
S	M	T	W	T	F	S
						1
2	3	4	5	6	7	8
9	10	11	12	13	14	15
16	17	18	19	20	21	22
23	24	25	26	27	28	29
30						

DECEMBER
S	M	T	W	T	F	S
	1	2	3	4	5	6
7	8	9	10	11	12	13
14	15	16	17	18	19	20
21	22	23	24	25	26	27
28	29	30	31			

Flip to the back for a look ahead with the 2026 Advance Planner.

January

GOALS AND DREAMS:

_____
_____
_____
_____
_____
_____
_____
_____
_____
_____
_____
_____
_____
_____
_____
_____
_____
_____
_____

No winter lasts forever; no spring skips its turn.
–Hal Borland, American journalist (1900–78)

SUNDAY	MONDAY	TUESDAY
5	6 *First Quarter* Epiphany	7 *Orthodox Christmas (Julian)*
12	13 *Full Wolf Moon*	14
19	20 *Martin Luther King Jr.'s Birthday, observed* *Inauguration Day*	21 *Last Quarter*
26	27	28

IT TAKES ABOUT 2 MONTHS TO CREATE A NEW HABIT. START NOW!

WEDNESDAY	THURSDAY	FRIDAY	SATURDAY
1 *New Year's Day*	2	3	4
8	9	10	11
15	16	17	18
22	23	24	25
29 ☆●☆ *New Moon* *Lunar New Year (China)*	30	31	

For more holidays, see the weekly pages that follow.

30 MONDAY

NEW MOON

31 TUESDAY

New Year's Eve

To remove the smell
of onions from your
hands, rub them
with dry mustard
and then wash.

1 WEDNESDAY

New Year's Day

For good luck, display a
new calendar only after
sunrise on January 1.

2 THURSDAY

A cat pent up
becomes a lion.
–Italian proverb

In a gentle way, you can shake the world.
–Mahatma Gandhi,
Indian spiritual leader
(1869–1948)

FRIDAY 3

Look north in
the predawn sky
for the Quadrantid
meteor shower.

SATURDAY 4

Q: What do sheep sing
on birthdays?

A: "Happy Birthday
to Ewe"

SUNDAY 5

REMINDERS

_____

_____

_____

_____

_____

_____

			JANUARY			
S	M	T	W	T	F	S
				1	2	3	4
5	6	7	8	9	10	11
12	13	14	15	16	17	18
19	20	21	22	23	24	25
26	27	28	29	30	31	

Complement this planner with daily weather and Almanac wit and wisdom at Almanac.com.

January

6 **MONDAY**

FIRST QUARTER

Epiphany

7 **TUESDAY**

Orthodox Christmas
(Julian)

Begonias do well in
light from an east- or
west-facing window.

8 **WEDNESDAY**

Elvis Presley's
Birthday

When rearranged, the
letters of "Elvis Aaron
Presley" spell "Seen
alive? Sorry, pal."

9 **THURSDAY**

*I merely took the
energy it takes to
pout and wrote
some blues.*
–Duke Ellington,
American bandleader
(1899–1974)

FRIDAY 10

The albedo, or
reflective ability,
of fresh snow is
typically between
80 percent and
90 percent.

SATURDAY 11

To reinvigorate
houseplants, remove
the top ¼ inch of soil
and top-dress with
fresh potting mix.

SUNDAY 12

If January could,
he would be a
summer month.
–Greek proverb

REMINDERS

JANUARY

S	M	T	W	T	F	S
				1	2	3	4
5	6	7	8	9	10	11
12	13	14	15	16	17	18
19	20	21	22	23	24	25
26	27	28	29	30	31	

Complement this planner with daily weather and Almanac wit and wisdom at Almanac.com.

January

13 MONDAY

FULL WOLF MOON

14 TUESDAY

The art of bell
ringing is called
campanology.

15 WEDNESDAY

On this day in 1932,
2 inches of snow
fell on Los Angeles,
California.

16 THURSDAY

According to tradition,
wood should be cut
in January during
the waning Moon.

FRIDAY 17

Benjamin Franklin's Birthday

Remember . . . to leave unsaid the wrong thing at the tempting moment.
–Benjamin Franklin,
American statesman
(1706–90)

SATURDAY 18

Today is lucky for those born under the sign of Capricorn (December 22– January 19).

SUNDAY 19

Better the cold blast of winter than the hot breath of a pursuing elephant.

REMINDERS

JANUARY

S	M	T	W	T	F	S
			1	2	3	4
5	6	7	8	9	10	11
12	13	14	15	16	17	18
19	20	21	22	23	24	25
26	27	28	29	30	31	

Complement this planner with daily weather and Almanac wit and wisdom at Almanac.com.

January

20 MONDAY

Martin Luther King Jr.'s Birthday, observed

Inauguration Day

At age 15, Martin Luther King Jr. enrolled at Morehouse College, the alma mater of his father and maternal grandfather.

21 TUESDAY

LAST QUARTER

22 WEDNESDAY

In January, when down the dairy The cream and clabber freeze, When snowdrifts cover the fences over, We farmers take our ease.

–Edmund Clarence Stedman, American poet (1833–1908)

23 THURSDAY

There are 86,400 seconds in a day.

Another reason to drink more water: Dehydration is a common cause of daytime fatigue.

FRIDAY 24

The name "chicken pox" may have come from the Old English term *gican pox*, which meant "itchy pox."

SATURDAY 25

Why is it that our feet smell and our nose runs?

SUNDAY 26

REMINDERS

JANUARY						
S	M	T	W	T	F	S
				1	2	3	4
5	6	7	8	9	10	11
12	13	14	15	16	17	18
19	20	21	22	23	24	25
26	27	28	29	30	31	

Complement this planner with daily weather and Almanac wit and wisdom at Almanac.com.

January–February

27 MONDAY

Waste not fresh tears over old griefs.
–Euripedes, Greek dramatist
(c. 484–406 B.C.)

28 TUESDAY

Prior to the Lunar New Year, celebrants traditionally give their homes a thorough cleaning to remove the old year's bad luck.

29 WEDNESDAY

NEW MOON

Lunar New Year (China)

30 THURSDAY

Make snow ice cream! Put several cups of clean, white snow into a cold bowl. Add a little sugar and a teaspoon of vanilla extract. Mix together and enjoy!

FRIDAY 31

Popular in the 19th century, poetry mittens had lines of verse woven into their design.

SATURDAY 1

First day of Black History Month

Stand for something, or you'll fall for anything. Today's mighty oak is yesterday's nut that held its ground.

–Rosa Parks, American civil rights activist (1913–2005)

SUNDAY 2

Candlemas

Groundhog Day

As far as the Sun shines in on Candlemas Day, So far will the snow blow in afore old May.

REMINDERS

_____

_____

_____

_____

_____

_____

FEBRUARY						
S	M	T	W	T	F	S
						1
2	3	4	5	6	7	8
9	10	11	12	13	14	15
16	17	18	19	20	21	22
23	24	25	26	27	28	

Complement this planner with daily weather and Almanac wit and wisdom at Almanac.com.

February

GOALS AND DREAMS:

_The February
sunshine steeps your
boughs and tints the
buds and swells the
leaves within._

–William Cullen Bryant,
American poet
(1794–1878)

SUNDAY	MONDAY	TUESDAY
2 _Candlemas_ _Groundhog Day_	3	4
9	10	11
16	17 _Presidents' Day_	18
23	24	25

DON'T ALLOW SMALL PROBLEMS TO BECOME BIG PROBLEMS.

WEDNESDAY	THURSDAY	FRIDAY	SATURDAY
			1 *First day of Black History Month*
5 ☾ *First Quarter*	**6**	**7**	**8**
12 ☽ *Full Snow Moon* *Abraham Lincoln's Birthday*	**13**	**14** *Valentine's Day*	**15** *National Flag of Canada Day*
19	**20** ☾ *Last Quarter*	**21**	**22** *George Washington's Birthday*
26	**27** ● *New Moon*	**28** *Ramadan begins at sundown*	

For more holidays, see the weekly pages that follow.

February

3 MONDAY

On this day in 1995,
Air Force Lt. Col.
Eileen Collins became
the first woman to
pilot a space shuttle
(Discovery).

4 TUESDAY

Sesquipedalophobia
is the fear of long
words.

5 WEDNESDAY

FIRST QUARTER

6 THURSDAY

Use a broom to gently
brush heavy snow
off evergreens.

FRIDAY 7

The flap of skin below a moose's throat is called a "bell" or "dewlap."

SATURDAY 8

Hungry? Grab a bite in Toast, North Carolina; Oatmeal, Texas; or Sandwich, Massachusetts.

SUNDAY 9

The road to success is lined with many tempting parking spaces.

REMINDERS

FEBRUARY

S	M	T	W	T	F	S
						1
2	3	4	5	6	7	8
9	10	11	12	13	14	15
16	17	18	19	20	21	22
23	24	25	26	27	28	

Complement this planner with daily weather and Almanac wit and wisdom at Almanac.com.

February

10 MONDAY

Fingernails grow nearly four times faster than toenails; the fastest are on your middle fingers.

11 TUESDAY

Today is lucky for those born under the sign of Aquarius (January 20– February 19).

12 WEDNESDAY

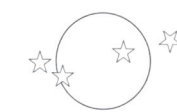

FULL SNOW MOON

Abraham Lincoln's Birthday

13 THURSDAY

By all means, don't say "If I can"; say "I will."
–Abraham Lincoln, 16th U.S. president (1809–65)

Valentine's Day

A happy heart is better
than a full purse.

FRIDAY 14

**National Flag of
Canada Day**

**Susan B. Anthony's
Birthday (Fla.)**

The name Susan
comes from the
Hebrew word
Shushannah,
meaning "lily of
the valley."

SATURDAY 15

*Lack of pep is often
mistaken for patience.*
–Kin Hubbard, American
humorist (1868–1930)

SUNDAY 16

REMINDERS

FEBRUARY						
S	M	T	W	T	F	S
						1
2	3	4	5	6	7	8
9	10	11	12	13	14	15
16	17	18	19	20	21	22
23	24	25	26	27	28	

February

17 MONDAY

Presidents' Day
**Family Day (Alta.,
B.C., N.B., Ont., Sask.)**

Four U.S. presidents
were born in
February—George
Washington, William
Henry Harrison,
Abraham Lincoln,
and Ronald Reagan.

18 TUESDAY

To dream that you have
laryngitis may indicate
that you should not take
unnecessary risks in the
next few weeks.

19 WEDNESDAY

Q: What is that which
was tomorrow and
will be yesterday?
A: Today

20 THURSDAY

LAST QUARTER

Heritage Day (Y.T.)

FRIDAY 21

North America's coldest temperature was recorded in Snag, Yukon Territory, in February 1947, when the mercury dropped to –81.4°F!

George Washington's Birthday

SATURDAY 22

George Washington's second inaugural address was the briefest in U.S. history, consisting of only 135 words.

Hold a true friend with both hands.
–Nigerian proverb

SUNDAY 23

REMINDERS

FEBRUARY

S	M	T	W	T	F	S
						1
2	3	4	5	6	7	8
9	10	11	12	13	14	15
16	17	18	19	20	21	22
23	24	25	26	27	28	

February–March

24 MONDAY

In 1984, a meteorite from Mars was found in Antarctica.

25 TUESDAY

A quarter-cup of maple syrup contains more calcium than the same amount of milk and more potassium than a banana.

26 WEDNESDAY

Knife falls, gentleman calls. Fork falls, lady calls. Spoon falls, baby squalls.

27 THURSDAY

NEW MOON

FRIDAY 28

Ramadan begins at sundown

Adding ¼ teaspoon of almond extract to cherry pie produces a richer flavor.

SATURDAY 1

Sun is showing,
Sap is flowing,
Flowers growing:
Whoops! It's snowing!
–The Old Farmer's Almanac, 1985

SUNDAY 2

Texas Independence Day

Texas is the only state that allows astronauts to legally cast absentee ballots from space.

REMINDERS

MARCH						
S	M	T	W	T	F	S
						1
2	3	4	5	6	7	8
9	10	11	12	13	14	15
16	17	18	19	20	21	22
23	24	25	26	27	28	29
30	31					

Complement this planner with daily weather and Almanac wit and wisdom at Almanac.com.

March

GOALS AND DREAMS:

_____
_____
_____
_____
_____
_____
_____
_____
_____
_____
_____
_____
_____
_____
_____

Happiness?
The color of it must
be spring green.
–Frances Mayes,
American writer
(b. 1940)

SUNDAY	MONDAY	TUESDAY
2	3 *Orthodox Lent begins*	4
9 *Daylight Saving Time begins at 2:00 A.M.*	10 *Commonwealth Day (Canada)*	11
16	17 *St. Patrick's Day*	18
23	24	25
30	31 *César Chávez Day*	

TAKE CARE OF YOUR BODY; IT'S THE ONLY ONE THAT YOU HAVE.

WEDNESDAY	THURSDAY	FRIDAY	SATURDAY
			1
5 *Ash Wednesday*	6 *First Quarter*	7	8 *International Women's Day*
12	13	14 *Full Worm Moon*	15
19	20 *Vernal Equinox*	21	22 *Last Quarter*
26	27	28	29 *New Moon*

For more holidays, see the weekly pages that follow.

March

3 MONDAY

Orthodox Lent begins

In the eyes of its mother, every turkey is a swan.

4 TUESDAY

Mardi Gras (Ala., La.)
Town Meeting Day (Vt.)

At 449 feet 5 inches, the longest wooden two-span covered bridge in the world connects Cornish, New Hampshire, and Windsor, Vermont.

5 WEDNESDAY

Ash Wednesday

March brings breezes loud and shrill, Stirs the dancing daffodil.
–Sara Coleridge, English poet (1802–52)

6 THURSDAY

FIRST QUARTER

FRIDAY 7

Before going to bed, arrange your shoes in the shape of a "T" to guard against nightmares.

SATURDAY 8

International Women's Day

In 1887, Susanna Madora Salter became the first elected woman mayor of an American community (Argonia, Kansas).

SUNDAY 9

Daylight Saving Time begins at 2:00 A.M.

Drive carefully: It takes about 1 week for our circadian rhythms to adjust to a 1-hour time loss.

REMINDERS

	MARCH					
S	M	T	W	T	F	S
						1
2	3	4	5	6	7	8
9	10	11	12	13	14	15
16	17	18	19	20	21	22
23	24	25	26	27	28	29
30	31					

Complement this planner with daily weather and Almanac wit and wisdom at Almanac.com.

March

10 MONDAY

Commonwealth Day (Canada)

Skating teaches you to do the things that you should do before you do the things that you want to do.

–Barbara Ann Scott, Canadian figure skater (1928–2012)

11 TUESDAY

Recycle flat club soda by using it to water houseplants.

12 WEDNESDAY

Today is lucky for those born under the sign of Pisces (February 20– March 20).

13 THURSDAY

Total Lunar Eclipse begins (visible in most of N.Am.)

Earthworms are capable of living up to 8 years.

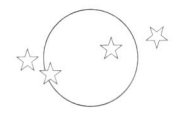

FULL WORM MOON

SATURDAY 15

In the ancient Roman lunar calendar, the "ides" were the 15th days of March, May, July, and October, and the 13th days of the other 6 months (there were only 10 at first).

SUNDAY 16

Unsalted butter is preferable to salted when baking, as it is usually sweeter and fresher and won't add more salt to the recipe.

REMINDERS

MARCH

S	M	T	W	T	F	S
						1
2	3	4	5	6	7	8
9	10	11	12	13	14	15
16	17	18	19	20	21	22
23	24	25	26	27	28	29
30	31					

March

17 MONDAY

St. Patrick's Day

Evacuation Day (Suffolk Co., Mass.)

The human eye can see more shades of green than any other color.

18 TUESDAY

Love is flower-like; friendship is like a sheltering tree.

–Samuel Taylor Coleridge, English poet (1772–1835)

19 WEDNESDAY

A group of squirrels is called a dray.

20 THURSDAY

Vernal Equinox

As the wind and weather at the equinoxes, so will they be for the next 3 months.

According to folklore,
  the last quarter
  Moon is a time
  for introspection.

SATURDAY 22

LAST QUARTER

SUNDAY 23

Who hath a book
Has but to read
And he may be
A king indeed.
–Wilbur D. Nesbit,
American poet
(1871–1927)

REMINDERS

			MARCH			
S	M	T	W	T	F	S
						1
2	3	4	5	6	7	8
9	10	11	12	13	14	15
16	17	18	19	20	21	22
23	24	25	26	27	28	29
30	31					

March

24 MONDAY

According to some studies, a zebra's stripes help to confuse biting flies.

25 TUESDAY

Fill your life with experiences, not excuses.

26 WEDNESDAY

Go for a walk in the woods to find the spring ephemerals (first wildflowers).

27 THURSDAY

The tin can for preserving food was invented in 1810—almost 50 years before the can opener (1858).

Like an army defeated,
The snow hath retreated.
–William Wordsworth,
English poet (1770–1850)

FRIDAY 28

NEW MOON

Partial Solar
Eclipse (visible in
parts of N.Am.)

SATURDAY 29

A brinicle is a hollow
tube of ice that grows
downward below
floating sea ice.

SUNDAY 30

REMINDERS

			MARCH			
S	M	T	W	T	F	S
						1
2	3	4	5	6	7	8
9	10	11	12	13	14	15
16	17	18	19	20	21	22
23	24	25	26	27	28	29
30	31					

31
MONDAY

César Chávez Day
Seward's Day
(Alaska)

You are never strong enough that you don't need help.
–César Chávez, American labor leader (1927–93)

1
TUESDAY

All Fools' Day

In France on this day, children secretly stick paper fish on the backs of people and shout "Poisson d'Avril!" ("April Fish!").

2
WEDNESDAY

Pascua Florida Day

Pelicans incubate their eggs by standing on them.

3
THURSDAY

Use a mixture of equal parts witch hazel and rubbing alcohol to massage sore muscles.

FIRST QUARTER

Today is lucky for
those born under
the sign of Aries
(March 21–April 20).

Till April's dead,
Change not a thread.

REMINDERS

APRIL

S	M	T	W	T	F	S
			1	2	3	4	5
6	7	8	9	10	11	12
13	14	15	16	17	18	19
20	21	22	23	24	25	26
27	28	29	30			

Complement this planner with daily weather and Almanac wit and wisdom at Almanac.com.

April

APRIL 12:
FULL PINK MOON

GOALS AND DREAMS:

_____
_____
_____
_____
_____
_____
_____
_____
_____
_____
_____
_____
_____
_____
_____
_____
_____

Gladness is born of
the April weather,
And the heart is
as light as a wind-
tossed feather.
–Eben Eugene Rexford,
American poet
(1848–1916)

SUNDAY	MONDAY	TUESDAY
		1 *All Fools' Day*
6	7	8
13 *Palm Sunday*	14	15
20 ☽ *Last Quarter* *Easter* *Orthodox Easter*	21 *Easter Monday*	22 *Earth Day*
27 ● *New Moon*	28	29

SHOP LOCAL: BY DOING SO, YOU ARE INVESTING IN YOUR COMMUNITY.

WEDNESDAY	THURSDAY	FRIDAY	SATURDAY
2	3	4 *First Quarter*	5
9	10	11	12 *Full Pink Moon* *Passover begins at sundown*
16	17	18 *Good Friday*	19
23 *Holocaust Remembrance Day begins at sundown*	24	25 *National Arbor Day*	26
30			

For more holidays, see the weekly pages that follow.

April

7 MONDAY

The largest cat found in the wild is the Siberian tiger, which can weigh 660 pounds and measure 11 feet long.

8 TUESDAY

To attract bumblebees and other bee species, consider putting native plants such as asters, coneflowers, lupines, and bee balm in your garden.

9 WEDNESDAY

Expect to laugh soon if your left eye itches.

10 THURSDAY

Winter's done, and April's in the skies, Earth, look up with laughter in your eyes!
–Sir Charles G. D. Roberts, Canadian poet (1860–1943)

FRIDAY 11

For the duration of Passover, observants refrain from consuming all leavened or fermented food or drink, including cake, cookies, cereal, pasta, and most alcoholic beverages.

SATURDAY 12

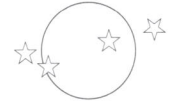

FULL PINK MOON

Passover begins at sundown

SUNDAY 13

Palm Sunday

Thomas Jefferson's Birthday

Thomas Jefferson is credited with introducing french fries to America.

REMINDERS

_____

_____

_____

_____

_____

APRIL

S	M	T	W	T	F	S
		1	2	3	4	5
6	7	8	9	10	11	12
13	14	15	16	17	18	19
20	21	22	23	24	25	26
27	28	29	30			

April

14 MONDAY

It's no use carrying an umbrella if your shoes are leaking.
–Irish proverb

15 TUESDAY

Keep centerpieces low so that guests can see each other across the table.

16 WEDNESDAY

For luck, keep in your pocket a coin from the year of your birth.

17 THURSDAY

Benjamin Franklin died on this day in 1790. An estimated 20,000 people—the largest gathering of its kind in Philadelphia history—would attend his funeral.

Good Friday

Parsley is said to germinate faster if planted on Good Friday.

Over the 500-year period from 1600 to 2099, Easter will have been celebrated most often on March 31 or April 16.

LAST QUARTER

Easter
Orthodox Easter

REMINDERS

APRIL

S	M	T	W	T	F	S
		1	2	3	4	5
6	7	8	9	10	11	12
13	14	15	16	17	18	19
20	21	22	23	24	25	26
27	28	29	30			

Complement this planner with daily weather and Almanac wit and wisdom at Almanac.com.

April

21 MONDAY

Easter Monday

Patriots Day
(Maine, Mass.)

San Jacinto Day
(Tex.)

St. George's Day,
observed (N.L.)

Plant your peas by
Patriots Day.

22 TUESDAY

Earth Day

*A morning glory at
my window satisfies
me more than the
metaphysics of books.*
–Walt Whitman,
American poet
(1819–92)

23 WEDNESDAY

Holocaust
Remembrance Day
begins at sundown

*Oh, memory's Sun
should never set!
Remember me—
do not forget.*
–Marion Manville Pope,
American poet
(1859–1930)

24 THURSDAY

Birthday of
Robert B. Thomas,
founder of *The Old
Farmer's Almanac*

Robert B. Thomas
published 54 editions
(1793–1846) of *The Old
Farmer's Almanac.*

National Arbor Day

Q: How do trees get on the Internet?

A: They log in.

When spring allergies hit, get relief by drinking hot or iced peppermint tea.

NEW MOON

REMINDERS

S	**M**	**T**	**W**	**T**	**F**	**S**
			1	2	3	4	5
6	7	8	9	10	11	12
13	14	15	16	17	18	19
20	21	22	23	24	25	26
27	28	29	30			

APRIL

Complement this planner with daily weather and Almanac wit and wisdom at Almanac.com.

28 MONDAY

When the chess game is
over, the pawns, rooks,
knights, bishops, kings,
and queens all go back
into the same box.
–Italian proverb

29 TUESDAY

Divide rhubarb every
3 to 6 years in early
spring or late fall.

30 WEDNESDAY

In Ireland on
the evening before
May Day, yellow
flowers such as
buttercups and
marigolds were
picked for May
baskets.

1 THURSDAY

**First day of Asian
American,
Native Hawaiian,
and Pacific Islander
Heritage Month**

May Day

Each Hawaiian island
has its own official
flower.

On this day in 1964, Northern Dancer—called a "runt" as a colt by prospective buyers—became the first Canadian horse to win the Kentucky Derby.

FRIDAY 2

When trout refuse
bait or fly,
There ever is a
storm nigh.

SATURDAY 3

SUNDAY 4

FIRST QUARTER

REMINDERS

	MAY					
S	M	T	W	T	F	S
					1	2	3
4	5	6	7	8	9	10
11	12	13	14	15	16	17
18	19	20	21	22	23	24
25	26	27	28	29	30	31

Complement this planner with daily weather and Almanac wit and wisdom at Almanac.com.

May

MAY 12:
FULL FLOWER MOON

GOALS AND DREAMS:

_____
_____
_____
_____
_____
_____
_____
_____
_____
_____
_____
_____
_____
_____
_____
_____
_____

There are flowers
everywhere for
those who want
to see them.
–Henri Matisse, French
artist (1869–1954)

SUNDAY	MONDAY	TUESDAY
4 *First Quarter*	5 *Cinco de Mayo*	6
11 *Mother's Day*	12 *Full Flower Moon*	13
18	19 *Victoria Day (Canada)*	20 *Last Quarter*
25	26 *New Moon* *Memorial Day, observed*	27

TAKE SEVERAL QUIET MINUTES EVERY DAY TO REFLECT, DE-STRESS, AND REFOCUS.

WEDNESDAY	THURSDAY	FRIDAY	SATURDAY
	1 *First day of Asian American, Native Hawaiian, and Pacific Islander Heritage Month* *May Day*	2	3
7	8	9	10
14	15	16	17 *Armed Forces Day*
21	22 *National Maritime Day*	23	24
28	29	30	31

For more holidays, see the weekly pages that follow.

May

5 MONDAY

Cinco de Mayo

Mole poblano is a complex chile-chocolate sauce traditionally eaten on this day in Mexico.

6 TUESDAY

The ancient Aztecs used cacao beans like money. A hen turkey was worth 100 beans; a turkey egg, three beans; and a large tomato, one bean.

7 WEDNESDAY

On this day in 1789, President George and First Lady Martha Washington hosted the first inaugural ball.

8 THURSDAY

Truman Day (Mo.)

Missouri's official state dinosaur is *Parrosaurus missouriensis.*

Today is lucky for
those born under
the sign of Taurus
(April 21–May 20).

FRIDAY 9

Apply honey to relieve
a canker sore's pain
and help it to heal.

SATURDAY 10

Mother's Day

The greatest love is a
mother's; then comes
a dog's; then comes
a sweetheart's.
–Polish proverb

SUNDAY 11

REMINDERS

MAY

S	M	T	W	T	F	S
				1	2	3
4	5	6	7	8	9	10
11	12	13	14	15	16	17
18	19	20	21	22	23	24
25	26	27	28	29	30	31

Complement this planner with daily weather and Almanac wit and wisdom at Almanac.com.

May

12 MONDAY

FULL FLOWER MOON

13 TUESDAY

After common lilac flowers fade, it is time to plant cucumbers and squash.

14 WEDNESDAY

May you live as long as you want
And never want as long as you live.
–Irish proverb

15 THURSDAY

When ants appear in the kitchen, place a few stems of mint, gently crushed, near suspected entry points.

Another glorious day,
the air as delicious to
the lungs as nectar to
the tongue.
–John Muir, Scottish-
born American naturalist
(1838–1914)

FRIDAY 16

Armed Forces Day

For tasty, iron-rich
salads, include
dandelion leaves
picked when they are
young and less bitter
than they will be later.

SATURDAY 17

The space between
the eyebrows, just
above the nose, is
the glabella.

SUNDAY 18

REMINDERS

MAY

S	M	T	W	T	F	S
				1	2	3
4	5	6	7	8	9	10
11	12	13	14	15	16	17
18	19	20	21	22	23	24
25	26	27	28	29	30	31

Complement this planner with daily weather and Almanac wit and wisdom at Almanac.com.

May

19 MONDAY

Victoria Day (Canada)

Canada's Victoria
Day—always on the
Monday before
May 25—serves as
the official observance
of the reigning
monarch's birthday.

20 TUESDAY

LAST QUARTER

21 WEDNESDAY

To remove a bandage
painlessly, dab it
with baby oil.

22 THURSDAY

National Maritime Day

A still river never finds
the ocean.

FRIDAY 23

Beet greens are
highly nutritious
and contain the
carotenoid pigments
beta-carotene, lutein,
and zeaxanthin,
which are important
for eye health.

SATURDAY 24

When washing
windows, use
horizontal and
vertical strokes on
opposite sides of
the glass so that
you'll know which
side has any streaks.

SUNDAY 25

*The only possible
guarantee of the future
is responsible behavior
in the present.*
–Wendell Berry,
American writer
(b. 1934)

MAY

REMINDERS

MAY						
S	M	T	W	T	F	S
				1	2	3
4	5	6	7	8	9	10
11	12	13	14	15	16	17
18	19	20	21	22	23	24
25	26	27	28	29	30	31

Complement this planner with daily weather and Almanac wit and wisdom at Almanac.com.

26 MONDAY

NEW MOON

**Memorial Day,
observed**

27 TUESDAY

Pink hydrangeas
retain their color
best in soil with a pH
greater than 6.0.

28 WEDNESDAY

In brevity lies delight.
–German proverb

29 THURSDAY

Since ancient times,
clean spiderwebs
have been used to
bind wounds.

MAY

FRIDAY 30

Control aphids by wiping or spraying the leaves of affected plants with a mild solution of water and a few drops of dish soap.

SATURDAY 31

Butterflies taste with their feet.

SUNDAY 1

First day of Pride Month

Canadian Armed Forces Day

Be you. Don't be someone else. You are a unique individual.

–Apolo Ohno, American Olympic speed skater (b. 1982)

REMINDERS

JUNE

S	M	T	W	T	F	S
1	2	3	4	5	6	7
8	9	10	11	12	13	14
15	16	17	18	19	20	21
22	23	24	25	26	27	28
29	30					

June

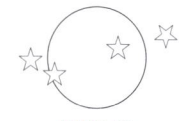

**JUNE 11:
FULL STRAWBERRY
MOON**

GOALS AND DREAMS:

_____

_____

_____

_____

_____

_____

_____

_____

_____

_____

_____

_____

_____

_____

_____

_____

*I wonder what it
would be like to live
in a world where it
was always June.*

–Lucy Maud
Montgomery, Canadian
writer (1874–1942)
in *Anne of the Island*

SUNDAY	MONDAY	TUESDAY
1 *First day of Pride Month*	2 *First Quarter*	3
8 *Whitsunday–Pentecost* *Orthodox Pentecost*	9	10
15 *Father's Day*	16	17
22	23	24
29	30	

GIVE SOMEONE YOUR UNDIVIDED ATTENTION: TURN OFF THE CELL PHONE OR TV.

WEDNESDAY	THURSDAY	FRIDAY	SATURDAY
4	5 *World Environment Day*	6 *D-Day*	7
11 ☆◐☆ *Full Strawberry Moon*	12	13	14 *Flag Day*
18 ☆◑☆ *Last Quarter*	19 *Juneteenth National Independence Day*	20 *Summer Solstice*	21 *National Indigenous Peoples Day (Canada)*
25 ☆●☆ *New Moon*	26 *First of Muharram begins at sundown*	27	28

For more holidays, see the weekly pages that follow.

June

2 MONDAY

FIRST QUARTER

3 TUESDAY

Today is lucky for those born under the sign of Gemini (May 21–June 20).

4 WEDNESDAY

He who pries into every cloud may be stricken with a thunderbolt.

5 THURSDAY

World Environment Day

To sleep while flying, an albatross can lock its wings in the open position.

D-Day

For compost tea,
mix together 1 part
compost and 5 parts
water. Set aside
for 1 week, then
strain and use to
water plants.

FRIDAY 6

*No human being,
however great or
powerful, was ever
so free as a fish.*
–John Ruskin, English
artist (1819–1900)

SATURDAY 7

Whitsunday–Pentecost
Orthodox Pentecost

Ideas should be clear and
chocolate thick.
–Spanish proverb

SUNDAY 8

REMINDERS

JUNE

S	M	T	W	T	F	S
1	2	3	4	5	6	7
8	9	10	11	12	13	14
15	16	17	18	19	20	21
22	23	24	25	26	27	28
29	30					

June

9 MONDAY

Hollyhocks were often grown near outbuildings, including the privy. This often prompted discreet, genteel ladies who needed to use it to ask to "see the hollyhocks."

10 TUESDAY

Don't wash strawberries until you are ready to eat or use them.

11 WEDNESDAY

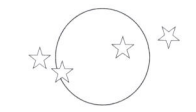

FULL STRAWBERY MOON

King Kamehameha I Day (Hawaii)

12 THURSDAY

In Hawaii, "pineapple juice" is a brief rain shower that occurs while the Sun is shining.

Each year has at least one Friday the 13th but no more than three. (This year, there's only one.)

FRIDAY 13

Flag Day
U.S. Army Birthday

In 1949, President Harry Truman established June 14 as national Flag Day.

SATURDAY 14

Father's Day

In Thailand, Father's Day is celebrated on the birthday of former King Bhumibol Adulyadej (1927–2016), December 5.

SUNDAY 15

REMINDERS

				JUNE		
S	M	T	W	T	F	S
1	2	3	4	5	6	7
8	9	10	11	12	13	14
15	16	17	18	19	20	21
22	23	24	25	26	27	28
29	30					

June

16 MONDAY

In the language of flowers, heliotrope, honeysuckle, hyacinth, white jasmine, roses, and yarrow all say "love."

17 TUESDAY

Bunker Hill Day (Suffolk Co., Mass.)

Lay red plastic mulch around tomato plants to hold in the soil's heat and increase productivity.

18 WEDNESDAY

LAST QUARTER

19 THURSDAY

Juneteenth National Independence Day

It is not light that we need, but fire; it is not the gentle shower, but thunder. We need the storm, the whirlwind, and the earthquake.

–Frederick Douglass, American abolitionist (1818–95)

FRIDAY 20

Summer Solstice
West Virginia Day

The northern cardinal is the state bird of Illinois, Indiana, Kentucky, North Carolina, Ohio, Virginia, and West Virginia.

SATURDAY 21

National Indigenous Peoples Day (Canada)

Today, Canadians celebrate the many achievements of the First Nations, Inuit, and Métis peoples.

SUNDAY 22

If there is a
rainbow at eve,
It will rain and leave.

REMINDERS

JUNE

S	M	T	W	T	F	S
1	2	3	4	5	6	7
8	9	10	11	12	13	14
15	16	17	18	19	20	21
22	23	24	25	26	27	28
29	30					

June

23 MONDAY

June Holiday (N.L.)

*Isn't it wonderful,
when you think,
How a little seed asleep,
Out of the earth new
life will drink,
And carefully
upward creep?*

–Julian Stearns Cutler,
American clergyman
(1854–1930)

24 TUESDAY

Fête Nationale (Qué.)

Quebec's flag, the "Fleurdelisé," consists of a blue field divided by a white cross into four quarters, each featuring a white fleur-de-lis.

25 WEDNESDAY

NEW MOON

26 THURSDAY

First of Muharram begins at sundown

Thin beets, carrots, parsnips, and onions to the point where you can get three fingers between individual plants.

Love this Old Farmer's Almanac Planner? Subscribe to receive one every year!

Sign up now, and each year along with your Planner we'll also send you
a free *Garden Guide* magazine—loaded with information
and inspiration for new and experienced gardeners alike (a $7.99 value)!

SIGN ME UP FOR THE OLD FARMER'S ALMANAC PLANNER SUBSCRIPTION!

This offer is available to U.S residents only.
We can not ship to Canada or other international addresses.

Your 2026 Planner and free gift will ship in August 2025. Every July thereafter, you'll receive
an advance notice of shipment for the next year's Planner, plus your free gift. You may use this advance
notice to change your address, change your order, or cancel the following year's shipment. You're under
no obligation to purchase future Planners and you may cancel your subscription at any time.

Name _____

Street _____

City _____ State _____ Zip _____

☐ Check enclosed

Charge my: ☐ Visa   ☐ MasterCard   ☐ AmEx   ☐ Discover

Card # _____ Exp. date _____ CVC _____

Signature _____
(Required for credit card orders)

Email _____ Phone _____

THE OLD FARMER'S ALMANAC PLANNER SUBSCRIPTION

Subscription price $ 16.99

Add state sales tax* $ _____

Shipping & handling $ 7.95

Total enclosed $ _____

*Residents of CT, IL, IN, MA, ME,
MI, OH, PA, UT, and WI: Please add
applicable sales tax.*

**MAIL THIS FORM WITH PAYMENT TO: THE OLD FARMER'S ALMANAC PLANNER,
P.O. BOX 37282, BOONE, IA 50037-0282
OR CALL: 1-800-ALMANAC (1-800-256-2622) AND SELECT OPTION 1**

Cut along dotted line.

H4JEGCP6

Name _____

Address _____

_____

City/Town _____ State _____ Zip _____

The Old Farmer's Almanac Planner
P.O. Box 37282
BOONE, IA 50037–0282

Fold along this line and seal all sides.

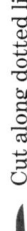

Cut along dotted line.

FRIDAY 27

A hummingbird has
a tongue twice as
long as its bill.

SATURDAY 28

It is not enough to
know how to ride:
You must also know
how to fall.
–Mexican proverb

SUNDAY 29

For decades, eggplant
was grown mainly for
decoration because it
was believed to cause
insanity if eaten.

REMINDERS

JUNE

S	M	T	W	T	F	S
1	2	3	4	5	6	7
8	9	10	11	12	13	14
15	16	17	18	19	20	21
22	23	24	25	26	27	28
29	30					

Complement this planner with daily weather and Almanac wit and wisdom at Almanac.com.

30 MONDAY

When it comes to
getting a sunburn,
ignorance is blister.

1 TUESDAY

Canada Day

*It is wonderful to
feel the grandness of
Canada in the raw.*
–Emily Carr,
Canadian artist
(1871–1945)

2 WEDNESDAY

FIRST QUARTER

3 THURSDAY

Those who wish to sing
always find a song.
–Swedish proverb

Independence Day
President Calvin
Coolidge (born on
this day in 1872) kept
a raccoon named
Rebecca as a pet.

FRIDAY 4

Seagull, seagull,
sit in the sand,
It's never good weather
when you're on the land.

SATURDAY 5

If you sleep on
your right side,
you generally have
pleasanter dreams
than if you sleep
on your left.

SUNDAY 6

REMINDERS

JULY

S	M	T	W	T	F	S
		1	2	3	4	5
6	7	8	9	10	11	12
13	14	15	16	17	18	19
20	21	22	23	24	25	26
27	28	29	30	31		

July

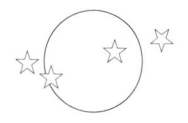

JULY 10:
FULL BUCK MOON

GOALS AND DREAMS:

_____
_____
_____
_____
_____
_____
_____
_____
_____
_____
_____
_____
_____
_____
_____
_____
_____
_____
_____

The summer night is like a perfection of thought.

–Wallace Stevens,
American poet
(1879–1955)

SUNDAY	MONDAY	TUESDAY
		1 *Canada Day*
6	7	8
13	14	15
20 *International Moon Day*	21	22
27	28	29

"PAY IT FORWARD": BUY COFFEE OR TEA FOR THE PERSON BEHIND YOU IN LINE.

WEDNESDAY	THURSDAY	FRIDAY	SATURDAY
2 ◐ *First Quarter*	3	4 *Independence Day*	5
9	10 *Full Buck Moon*	11	12
16	17 ◑ *Last Quarter*	18	19
23	24 ● *New Moon*	25	26 *National Day of the Cowboy*
30	31		

JULY

For more holidays, see the weekly pages that follow.

July

7 MONDAY

Today is lucky for
those born under the
sign of Cancer
(June 21–July 22).

8 TUESDAY

*Like a welcome summer
rain, humor may
suddenly cleanse and
cool the earth, the
air, and you.*
–Langston Hughes,
American poet (1902–67)

9 WEDNESDAY

Nunavut Day (Canada)

Iqaluit, the capital
of Nunavut, means
"place of many fish"
in Inuktitut.

10 THURSDAY

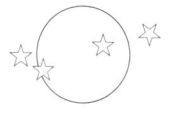

FULL BUCK MOON

According to one study, a full Moon increases mosquito activity by 500 percent.

FRIDAY 11

On this day in 2011, Neptune completed its first orbit around the Sun since its discovery in 1846.

SATURDAY 12

Triskaidekaphilia is the belief that the number 13 is lucky.

SUNDAY 13

REMINDERS

JULY
S M T W T F S
1 2 3 4 5
6 7 8 9 10 11 12
13 14 15 16 17 18 19
20 21 22 23 24 25 26
27 28 29 30 31

Complement this planner with daily weather and Almanac wit and wisdom at Almanac.com.

July

14 MONDAY

Orangemen's Day, observed (N.L.)

Woodchucks are as fond of the fruit of our gardens as we are, and even better at harvesting them.

–Ruth Page, American dancer (1899–1991)

15 TUESDAY

To prevent tough skins on blueberries, do not rinse them before freezing.

16 WEDNESDAY

When black snails on the road you see, Then on the morrow rain will be.

17 THURSDAY

LAST QUARTER

FRIDAY 18

Honey's anti-inflammatory properties may help with itch relief from bug bites.

SATURDAY 19

On the way to your wedding, it is good luck to meet a chimney sweep, elephant, or toad.

SUNDAY 20

International Moon Day

We came in peace for all mankind.

–Moon plaque inscription left on the Moon by Apollo 11 astronauts in 1969

REMINDERS

JULY

S	M	T	W	T	F	S
		1	2	3	4	5
6	7	8	9	10	11	12
13	14	15	16	17	18	19
20	21	22	23	24	25	26
27	28	29	30	31		

July

21 MONDAY

A summer's day
palindrome: It's
"too hot to hoot."

22 TUESDAY

To encourage a
cutting to root, add
a pinch of sugar
to the water.

23 WEDNESDAY

*All the night has voices.
But sometimes,
suddenly,
It grows so quiet
I know the world
Is listening with me.*
–"Summer Night," by
Benjamin Rice, American
writer (1903–78)

24 THURSDAY

NEW MOON

Pioneer Day (Utah)

Sow your turnips
the 25th of July,
You'll make a crop,
wet or dry.

FRIDAY 25

**National Day of
the Cowboy**

Q: What do you call
the horse that
lives next door?

A: Your neigh-bor.

SATURDAY 26

Your arm is about
10 times longer than
the distance between
your eyes.

SUNDAY 27

REMINDERS

JULY

S	M	T	W	T	F	S
		1	2	3	4	5
6	7	8	9	10	11	12
13	14	15	16	17	18	19
20	21	22	23	24	25	26
27	28	29	30	31		

28 MONDAY

Advice after mischief is
like medicine after death.
–Danish proverb

29 TUESDAY

If bats fly into the house,
expect rain.

30 WEDNESDAY

Ease a headache
by drinking tomato
juice blended with
fresh basil.

31 THURSDAY

*Knowledge is proud
that he has learned
so much;
Wisdom is humble that
he knows no more.*
–William Cowper, English
poet (1731–1800)

FIRST QUARTER

FRIDAY 1

Emancipation Day
(Canada)
Colorado Day

People in homes
filled with plants
suffer fewer
respiratory illnesses
and headaches.

SATURDAY 2

Today is lucky for
those born under
the sign of Leo
(July 23–August 22).

SUNDAY 3

REMINDERS

_____

_____

_____

_____

_____

_____

AUGUST

S	M	T	W	T	F	S
					1	2
3	4	5	6	7	8	9
10	11	12	13	14	15	16
17	18	19	20	21	22	23
24	25	26	27	28	29	30
31						

Complement this planner with daily weather and Almanac wit and wisdom at Almanac.com.

August

**AUGUST 9:
FULL STURGEON
MOON**

GOALS AND DREAMS:

_____
_____
_____
_____
_____
_____
_____
_____
_____
_____
_____
_____
_____
_____

Let us be grateful to people who make us happy; they are the charming gardeners who make our souls blossom.

–Marcel Proust, French writer (1871–1922)

SUNDAY	MONDAY	TUESDAY
3	4 Civic Holiday (Canada)	5
10	11	12
17	18	19 National Aviation Day
24	25	26
31 First Quarter		Women's Equality Day

SEEK OUT THE GOOD NEWS.

WEDNESDAY	THURSDAY	FRIDAY	SATURDAY
		1 *First Quarter* *Emancipation Day (Canada)*	2
6	7	8	9 *Full Sturgeon Moon*
13	14	15	16 *Last Quarter*
20	21	22	23 *New Moon*
27	28	29	30

For more holidays, see the weekly pages that follow.

August

4 MONDAY

If the first week in August is unusually warm, the winter will be white and long.

5 TUESDAY

For relief from indigestion, eat papaya or kiwi.

6 WEDNESDAY

Some people can stay longer in an hour than others can in a week.
–William Dean Howells, American writer (1837–1920)

7 THURSDAY

Prevent ice cream drips by putting a miniature marshmallow in the bottom of a sugar cone.

For best flavor, dig
horseradish during
the full Moon.

FRIDAY 8

SATURDAY 9

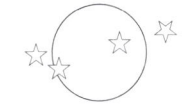

FULL STURGEON MOON

To dig a tunnel from
the Americas straight
through the center of
Earth to China, you'd
have to start from
Argentina or Chile. If
you tried from most of
North America, you'd
end up in the ocean.

SUNDAY 10

AUGUST

REMINDERS

AUGUST

S	M	T	W	T	F	S
					1	2
3	4	5	6	7	8	9
10	11	12	13	14	15	16
17	18	19	20	21	22	23
24	25	26	27	28	29	30
31						

Complement this planner with daily weather and Almanac wit and wisdom at Almanac.com.

August

11 MONDAY

The Perseid meteor shower peaks over the next few nights.

12 TUESDAY

On this day in 1981, IBM introduced both its personal computer and the operating system PC-DOS version 1.0.

13 WEDNESDAY

Candles stored in the refrigerator will drip and smoke less and burn longer.

14 THURSDAY

If bees stay at home,
Rain will soon come;
If they fly away,
Fine will be the day.

Seaweed is an excellent fertilizer for citrus trees and roses.

FRIDAY 15

LAST QUARTER

Bennington Battle Day (Vt.)

SATURDAY 16

The swiftlet bird employs its own saliva to build its nest, which cooks use to make the Chinese delicacy bird's nest soup.

SUNDAY 17

REMINDERS

AUGUST

S	M	T	W	T	F	S
					1	2
3	4	5	6	7	8	9
10	11	12	13	14	15	16
17	18	19	20	21	22	23
24	25	26	27	28	29	30
31						

Complement this planner with daily weather and Almanac wit and wisdom at Almanac.com.

August

18 MONDAY

Discovery Day (Y.T.)

When it rains in August, it
rains honey and wine.
–Spanish proverb

19 TUESDAY

National Aviation Day

NASA's vehicle
assembly building
is so big that it has
its own weather: If
the air-conditioning
is off on humid days,
mist can form inside.

20 WEDNESDAY

After a big meal, a
great white shark
needs no more food
for 2 months.

21 THURSDAY

Scientists estimate
that a single ragweed
plant can release
1 billion grains of
pollen over the
course of a season.

Life is like the Moon—
   now dark, now full.

FRIDAY 22

NEW MOON

SATURDAY 23

Thunderstorms after
St. Bartholomew's Day
[today] are more violent.

SUNDAY 24

REMINDERS

AUGUST

S	M	T	W	T	F	S
					1	2
3	4	5	6	7	8	9
10	11	12	13	14	15	16
17	18	19	20	21	22	23
24	25	26	27	28	29	30
31						

Complement this planner with daily weather and Almanac wit and wisdom at Almanac.com.

August

25 **MONDAY**

If you dream of a hedgehog, you'll see an old friend soon.

26 **TUESDAY**

Women's Equality Day

Life is meant to be lived, and curiosity must be kept alive.

–Eleanor Roosevelt, American humanitarian and first lady (1884–1962)

27 **WEDNESDAY**

Each of your feet has about 250,000 sweat glands.

28 **THURSDAY**

Q: Why did the scarecrow win the Nobel Prize?

A: Because it was out standing in its field.

To add great taste
to vegetables like
baby carrots, sliced
zucchini, and trimmed
green beans, marinate
them overnight
in leftover pickle
jar brine.

FRIDAY 29

When the stars begin
to huddle,
The earth will soon
become a puddle.

SATURDAY 30

SUNDAY 31

FIRST QUARTER

AUGUST

REMINDERS

SEPTEMBER

S	M	T	W	T	F	S
	1	2	3	4	5	6
7	8	9	10	11	12	13
14	15	16	17	18	19	20
21	22	23	24	25	26	27
28	29	30				

Complement this planner with daily weather and Almanac wit and wisdom at Almanac.com.

September

SEPTEMBER 7:
FULL CORN MOON

GOALS AND DREAMS:

_____

_____

_____

_____

_____

_____

_____

_____

_____

_____

_____

_____

_____

_____

_____

_____

_____

Enjoy your own life
without comparing it
with that of another.

–Marquis de Condorcet,
French philosopher
(1743–94)

SUNDAY	MONDAY	TUESDAY
	1 *Labor Day*	**2**
7 ☆☽☆ *Full Corn Moon* *Grandparents Day*	**8**	**9**
14 ◑ *Last Quarter*	**15** *First day of National Hispanic/Latinx Heritage Month*	**16**
21 ● *New Moon* *International Day of Peace*	**22** *Rosh Hashanah begins at sundown* *Autumnal Equinox*	**23**
28	**29** ◐ *First Quarter*	**30** *National Day for Truth and Reconciliation (Canada)*

WORK FOR A CAUSE, NOT FOR APPLAUSE.

WEDNESDAY	THURSDAY	FRIDAY	SATURDAY
3	4	5	6
10	11 *Patriot Day*	12	13
17 *Constitution Day*	18	19	20
24	25	26	27

SEPTEMBER

For more holidays, see the weekly pages that follow.

September

1 MONDAY

Labor Day

The 2026 Old Farmer's Almanac is available now.

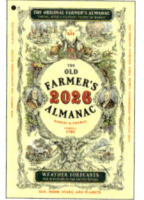

2 TUESDAY

Make not your sauce till you have caught the fish.

–English proverb

3 WEDNESDAY

To discourage squirrels, start a few garlic cloves near fall-planted spring bulbs.

4 THURSDAY

A garden rake falling over with its tines pointing upward means that rain is on the way.

FRIDAY 5

Yellow fruit and vegetables are loaded with beta-carotene, flavonoids, lycopene, potassium, and vitamin C.

SATURDAY 6

Saturdays are propitious for setting sail.

SUNDAY 7

FULL CORN MOON

Grandparents Day
Total Lunar Eclipse
(not visible in most of N.Am.)

REMINDERS

SEPTEMBER

S	M	T	W	T	F	S
	1	2	3	4	5	6
7	8	9	10	11	12	13
14	15	16	17	18	19	20
21	22	23	24	25	26	27
28	29	30				

September

8 MONDAY

Treasure the love [that] you receive above all. It will survive long after your good health has vanished.

–Og Mandino, American writer (1923–96)

9 TUESDAY

Admission Day (Calif.)

The world's largest living single-trunk tree is the General Sherman Tree, a giant sequoia in Sequoia National Park, California.

10 WEDNESDAY

Today is lucky for those born under the sign of Virgo (August 23–September 22).

11 THURSDAY

Patriot Day

Peace flourishes when reason rules.

–American proverb

FRIDAY 12

Seed new lawns
before the leaves fall.

SATURDAY 13

Patience is a bitter plant,
  but it has sweet fruit.
  –German proverb

SUNDAY 14

LAST QUARTER

SEPTEMBER

REMINDERS

SEPTEMBER						
S	M	T	W	T	F	S
	1	2	3	4	5	6
7	8	9	10	11	12	13
14	15	16	17	18	19	20
21	22	23	24	25	26	27
28	29	30				

Complement this planner with daily weather and Almanac wit and wisdom at Almanac.com.

September

15 MONDAY

First day of National Hispanic/Latinx Heritage Month

National Hispanic Heritage Week, which began as 7 days in 1968, was renamed and extended to be a monthlong celebration in 1988.

16 TUESDAY

To the brave man, every land is a native country.

17 WEDNESDAY

Constitution Day

The Constitution is the guide which I never will abandon.

–George Washington, 1st U.S. president (1732–99)

18 THURSDAY

U.S. Air Force Birthday

Kite-flying was an unofficial event at the 1900 Olympic Games in Paris.

Tweed: call issued by a
bird with a head cold

FRIDAY 19

For greater success, begin
ventures with the new
Moon (tomorrow).

SATURDAY 20

SUNDAY 21

NEW MOON

**International Day
of Peace**

**Partial Solar Eclipse
(not visible in N.Am.)**

REMINDERS

SEPTEMBER

S	M	T	W	T	F	S
		1	2	3	4	5	6
7	8	9	10	11	12	13
14	15	16	17	18	19	20
21	22	23	24	25	26	27
28	29	30				

September

22 MONDAY

Rosh Hashanah begins at sundown

Autumnal Equinox

At the autumnal equinox in Europe centuries ago, festivals known as Harvest Home marked and celebrated the end of the growing season.

23 TUESDAY

When translated into English, the Japanese word *edamame* means "branch bean."

24 WEDNESDAY

We blink about 15 to 20 times every minute and more rapidly when we are nervous or see something unpleasant.

25 THURSDAY

There is no room for two feet in one shoe.
–Greek proverb

When a hippo is under
water, its ears shut
and it hears through
its lower jawbone,
which conducts
sound waves.

*Years may wrinkle the
skin, but to give up
enthusiasm wrinkles
the soul.*

–Samuel Ullman, German-
born poet (1840–1924)

Substitute cold milk
for water in your
favorite piecrust
recipe. The result
will be a flaky crust
that browns evenly.

SEPTEMBER

REMINDERS

SEPTEMBER						
S	M	T	W	T	F	S
	1	2	3	4	5	6
7	8	9	10	11	12	13
14	15	16	17	18	19	20
21	22	23	24	25	26	27
28	29	30				

September–October

29 MONDAY

FIRST QUARTER

30 TUESDAY

National Day for Truth and Reconciliation (Canada)

We have been created for greater things, to love and be loved.

–Saint Teresa of Calcutta, Albanian humanitarian (1910–97)

1 WEDNESDAY

Yom Kippur begins at sundown

Speak little and do much.

–Hebrew proverb

2 THURSDAY

Stained your fingers with beet juice? Rub them clean with fresh lemon juice.

One day in the country is worth a month in town.

–Christina Rossetti, English poet (1830–94)

FRIDAY 3

To deodorize stinky sneakers, sprinkle coarse salt inside them, wait 24 hours, and then shake it out.

SATURDAY 4

A new broom sweeps clean, but the old brush knows all the corners.

SUNDAY 5

REMINDERS

OCTOBER

S	M	T	W	T	F	S
				1	2	3	4
5	6	7	8	9	10	11
12	13	14	15	16	17	18
19	20	21	22	23	24	25
26	27	28	29	30	31	

October

**OCTOBER 6:
FULL HARVEST MOON**

GOALS AND DREAMS:

_____

_____

_____

_____

_____

_____

_____

_____

_____

_____

_____

_____

_____

_____

_____

_____

_____

*When you reach for
the stars, you may not
quite get one, but you
won't come up with a
handful of mud either.*
–Leo Burnett, American
businessman (1891–1971)

SUNDAY	MONDAY	TUESDAY
5	6 *Full Harvest Moon* *Child Health Day*	7
12 *National Farmer's Day*	13 *Last Quarter* *Columbus Day, observed* *Indigenous Peoples' Day* *Thanksgiving Day (Canada)*	14
19	20	21 *New Moon*
26	27	28

WHEN TRYING NEW THINGS, ACCEPT THAT AT FIRST YOU MIGHT FAIL.

WEDNESDAY	THURSDAY	FRIDAY	SATURDAY
1 *Yom Kippur begins at sundown*	2	3	4
8	9 *Leif Eriksson Day*	10	11
15	16	17	18
22	23	24 *United Nations Day*	25
29 ☽ *First Quarter*	30	31 *Halloween*	

For more holidays, see the weekly pages that follow.

October

6 MONDAY

FULL HARVEST MOON

Child Health Day

7 TUESDAY

A party without cake is just a meeting.
–Julia Child, American culinary expert (1912–2004)

8 WEDNESDAY

Even a small star shines in the darkness.
–Danish proverb

9 THURSDAY

Leif Eriksson Day

Vikings likely never wore the horned helmets in which they are often portrayed.

FRIDAY 10

Scalded milk will be less likely to stick if it is heated in a pan prechilled in cold water.

SATURDAY 11

To improve the growth and leaf color of houseplants, feed them with a solution of a few drops of ammonia mixed into 1 quart of water.

SUNDAY 12

National Farmer's Day

Evenings will give the farmer time to take part in the games and entertainments of the children before their bedtime.

–*The Old Farmer's Almanac,* 1901

REMINDERS

OCTOBER

S	M	T	W	T	F	S
			1	2	3	4
5	6	7	8	9	10	11
12	13	14	15	16	17	18
19	20	21	22	23	24	25
26	27	28	29	30	31	

OCTOBER

October

13 MONDAY

LAST QUARTER

Columbus Day, observed
Indigenous Peoples' Day
U.S. Navy Birthday
Thanksgiving Day (Canada)

14 TUESDAY

In Newfoundland, it is traditional to eat Jiggs' dinner (salt beef boiled with cabbage and other vegetables) on Thanksgiving Day (Oct. 13 this year).

15 WEDNESDAY

Cover crops planted in cleared vegetable gardens will protect the soil until you're ready to plant again.

16 THURSDAY

Kindness in words creates confidence. Kindness in thinking creates profoundness. Kindness in giving creates love.

–Lao Tzu, Chinese philosopher (601–531 B.C.)

Today is lucky for those born under the sign of Libra (September 23–October 22).

FRIDAY 17

Alaska Day

To the lover of wilderness, Alaska is one of the most wonderful countries in the world.

–John Muir, Scottish-born American naturalist (1839–1914)

SATURDAY 18

Once iris foliage is hit with a heavy frost, remove and destroy it to eliminate borer eggs.

SUNDAY 19

REMINDERS

OCTOBER

S	M	T	W	T	F	S
			1	2	3	4
5	6	7	8	9	10	11
12	13	14	15	16	17	18
19	20	21	22	23	24	25
26	27	28	29	30	31	

OCTOBER

October

20 MONDAY

In the early 1800s, advertisements claimed that riding a carousel was good for blood circulation.

21 TUESDAY

NEW MOON

22 WEDNESDAY

According to weather lore, the days following a new Moon are typically stormy.

23 THURSDAY

The noblest art is that of making others happy.
–P. T. Barnum, American entrepreneur (1810–91)

United Nations Day

Onion skins thick
and tough,
Coming winter, cold
and rough.

"Nightmare" derives
from the Old English
word *mare,* which
represented a
monster or spirit
whose nighttime
visits made sleepers
feel as though they
were suffocating.

*One of the virtues of
being very young is that
you don't let the facts
get in the way of your
imagination.*

–Samuel Levenson,
American humorist
(1911–80)

REMINDERS

_____

_____

_____

_____

_____

OCTOBER

S	M	T	W	T	F	S
			1	2	3	4
5	6	7	8	9	10	11
12	13	14	15	16	17	18
19	20	21	22	23	24	25
26	27	28	29	30	31	

OCTOBER

Complement this planner with daily weather and Almanac wit and wisdom at Almanac.com.

27 MONDAY

Suck on an ice cube
before you take bad-
tasting medicine.

28 TUESDAY

On this day in 1886,
the Statue of Liberty
was unveiled in
New York Harbor.

29 WEDNESDAY

FIRST QUARTER

30 THURSDAY

On Thursday at three,
Look out, and you'll see
What Friday will be.

Halloween

Nevada Day

Q: What do you call a
haunting chicken?

A: A poultry-geist.

FRIDAY
31

---

*November comes
And November goes,
With the last red berries
And the first white
snows.*
–Elizabeth Coatsworth,
American writer
(1893–1986)

SATURDAY
1

**Daylight Saving Time
ends at 2:00 A.M.**

The clock strikes
differently every hour.
–Hindustani proverb

SUNDAY
2

REMINDERS

_____

_____

_____

_____

_____

_____

NOVEMBER

S	M	T	W	T	F	S
						1
2	3	4	5	6	7	8
9	10	11	12	13	14	15
16	17	18	19	20	21	22
23	24	25	26	27	28	29
30						

OCTOBER

Complement this planner with daily weather and Almanac wit and wisdom at Almanac.com.

November

NOVEMBER 5:
FULL BEAVER MOON

GOALS AND DREAMS:

_____
_____
_____
_____
_____
_____
_____
_____
_____
_____
_____
_____
_____
_____
_____
_____
_____

The soft November
days are here,
The aftermath of
blossom's year.

–Sara Louisa
Oberholtzer, American
poet (1841–1930)

SUNDAY	MONDAY	TUESDAY
2 *Daylight Saving Time ends at 2:00 A.M.*	3	4 *Election Day*
9	10	11 *Veterans Day* *Remembrance Day (Canada)*
16	17	18
23 30	24	25

BRING PLANTS INTO YOUR HOME TO HELP RELIEVE STRESS AND PURIFY THE AIR.

WEDNESDAY	THURSDAY	FRIDAY	SATURDAY
			1
5 ☆◑☆ *Full Beaver Moon*	6	7	8
12 ☆◐☆ *Last Quarter*	13	14	15
19 *Discovery of Puerto Rico Day*	20 ●☆ *New Moon*	21	22
26	27 *Thanksgiving Day*	28 ☆◗☆ *First Quarter*	29

NOVEMBER

For more holidays, see the weekly pages that follow.

National Child Day (Canada)

November

3 MONDAY

Cabbage is packed with immunity-boosting phytochemicals that are not damaged by cooking.

4 TUESDAY

Election Day

Will Rogers Day (Okla.)

Half our life is spent trying to find something to do with the time we have rushed through life trying to save.

–Will Rogers, American humorist (1879–1935)

5 WEDNESDAY

FULL BEAVER MOON

6 THURSDAY

Today is lucky for those born under the sign of Scorpio (October 23– November 22).

If decreased sunlight is making you drowsy, eat apples, apricots, grapes, oranges, or pears.

FRIDAY 7

When ducks stand on one leg, expect cold weather.

SATURDAY 8

According to tradition, fence posts should be set during the dark of the Moon (between full and new) to resist rotting.

SUNDAY 9

REMINDERS

NOVEMBER

S	M	T	W	T	F	S
						1
2	3	4	5	6	7	8
9	10	11	12	13	14	15
16	17	18	19	20	21	22
23	24	25	26	27	28	29
30						

NOVEMBER

November

10 MONDAY

U.S. Marine Corps Birthday

Nothing will work unless you do.

–Maya Angelou, American writer and poet (1928–2014)

11 TUESDAY

Veterans Day

Remembrance Day (Canada)

Before 1954, Veterans Day was known as Armistice Day.

12 WEDNESDAY

LAST QUARTER

13 THURSDAY

National Kindness Day

Kindness, like grain, increases by sowing.

To prevent meat loaf from sticking to the pan, place two strips of bacon on the bottom before adding the meat mixture.

FRIDAY 14

Books are not made for furniture, but there is nothing else that so beautifully furnishes a house.
–Henry Ward Beecher, American clergyman (1813–87)

SATURDAY 15

Vanilla is made from the fruit ("bean") of the vanilla orchid.

SUNDAY 16

REMINDERS

NOVEMBER

S	M	T	W	T	F	S
						1
2	3	4	5	6	7	8
9	10	11	12	13	14	15
16	17	18	19	20	21	22
23	24	25	26	27	28	29
30						

NOVEMBER

November

17 MONDAY

In Italy, 17 is an unlucky number. In most hotels, there is no 17th floor and no room 17.

18 TUESDAY

The grand thing in the world is not so much where we stand as in what direction we are moving.

–Oliver Wendell Holmes, American writer (1809–94)

19 WEDNESDAY

Discovery of Puerto Rico Day

The Puerto Rico Trench is the deepest part of the Atlantic Ocean.

20 THURSDAY

NEW MOON

National Child Day (Canada)

Not all birds head
south for the winter,
so consider a heated
birdbath if you're
in an area that
experiences cold.

FRIDAY 21

Penny after penny laid
up will be many.

SATURDAY 22

When applied to the
skin, calendula petals
will calm redness
and irritation.

SUNDAY 23

REMINDERS

_____

_____

_____

_____

_____

NOVEMBER						
S	M	T	W	T	F	S
						1
2	3	4	5	6	7	8
9	10	11	12	13	14	15
16	17	18	19	20	21	22
23	24	25	26	27	28	29
30						

NOVEMBER

November

24 MONDAY

Good judgment comes from experience, and a lot of that comes from bad judgment.

25 TUESDAY

Freshen sponges by soaking them overnight in a solution of 1 part vinegar and 2 parts water.

26 WEDNESDAY

To cure insomnia, drink warm milk that has been simmered with chopped garlic.

27 THURSDAY

Thanksgiving Day

*What moistens the lip
and what brightens
the eye?
What calls back the
past, like the rich
Pumpkin pie?*

–John Greenleaf Whittier,
American poet (1807–92)

FRIDAY 28

FIRST QUARTER

Acadian Day (La.)

SATURDAY 29

New Zealand's
national bird, the
kiwi, is the only fowl
with nostrils at the
end of its beak.

SUNDAY 30

The winds of the daytime
wrestle and fight
Longer and stronger
than those of the night.

REMINDERS

DECEMBER

S	M	T	W	T	F	S
	1	2	3	4	5	6
7	8	9	10	11	12	13
14	15	16	17	18	19	20
21	22	23	24	25	26	27
28	29	30	31			

NOVEMBER

Complement this planner with daily weather and Almanac wit and wisdom at Almanac.com.

December

GOALS AND DREAMS:

In seedtime, learn;
in harvest, teach;
in winter, enjoy.
–William Blake, English
poet (1757–1827)

SUNDAY	MONDAY	TUESDAY
	1	2
7 _National Pearl Harbor Remembrance Day_	8	9
14 _Chanukah begins at sundown_	15 _Bill of Rights Day_	16
21 _Winter Solstice_	22	23
28	29	30

STUDIES SHOW THAT SAYING "THANK YOU" CAN LEAD TO A HAPPIER LIFE.

WEDNESDAY	THURSDAY	FRIDAY	SATURDAY
3	4 *Full Cold Moon*	5	6
10	11 *Last Quarter*	12	13
17 *Wright Brothers Day*	18	19 *New Moon*	20
24	25 *Christmas Day*	26 *Boxing Day (Canada)* *First day of Kwanzaa*	27 *First Quarter*
31 *New Year's Eve*			

Complement this planner with daily weather and Almanac wit and wisdom at Almanac.com.

DECEMBER

December

1 MONDAY

*"We are nearer
to Spring
Than we were in
September,"
I heard a bird sing
In the dark of December.*
–Oliver Herford, English-
born American writer
(1863–1935)

2 TUESDAY

Use clothespins to
hang kids' artwork
on fishing line strung
along a playroom or
family room wall.

3 WEDNESDAY

Today is lucky for
those born under the
sign of Sagittarius
(November 23–
December 21).

4 THURSDAY

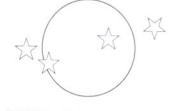

FULL COLD MOON

Only two breeds
of dog have black
tongues, the chow
chow and the shar-pei.

FRIDAY 5

For a soothing soak,
add herbal tea bags
to a tub full of warm
water. Chamomile,
peppermint, and
lavender are all
good choices.

SATURDAY 6

**National Pearl Harbor
Remembrance Day**

In Hindu folklore,
dewdrops that fell
from the Moon into
the sea became pearls.

SUNDAY 7

REMINDERS

			DECEMBER			
S	M	T	W	T	F	S
	1	2	3	4	5	6
7	8	9	10	11	12	13
14	15	16	17	18	19	20
21	22	23	24	25	26	27
28	29	30	31			

December

8

MONDAY

"First cousins" are children of two siblings. A "first cousin once removed" is your parent's first cousin or your first cousin's child.

9

TUESDAY

Quote me as saying I was misquoted.
–Groucho Marx, American actor (1890–1977)

10

WEDNESDAY

Welcome is the best dish in the kitchen.

11

THURSDAY

LAST QUARTER

A few drops of wintergreen oil in recycling bins and trash cans will freshen the air.

FRIDAY 12

U.S. National Guard Birthday

On this day in 1962, a severe Florida freeze damaged fruit trees: Tampa registered 18°F and Jacksonville, 12°F.

SATURDAY 13

Chanukah begins at sundown

"Chanukah" means "dedication" in Hebrew.

SUNDAY 14

REMINDERS

DECEMBER

S	M	T	W	T	F	S
	1	2	3	4	5	6
7	8	9	10	11	12	13
14	15	16	17	18	19	20
21	22	23	24	25	26	27
28	29	30	31			

December

15 MONDAY

Bill of Rights Day

James Madison,
who would later
become the fourth
U.S. president,
penned what is now
known as the Bill of
Rights, introducing
the amendments to
Congress in 1789.

16 TUESDAY

*If the only prayer you
said in your whole life
was "Thank you,"
that would suffice.*

–Meister Eckhart, German
theologian (1260–c. 1327)

17 WEDNESDAY

Wright Brothers Day

The Wright brothers
flew together
only once.

18 THURSDAY

*Of all the trees that are
in the wood, the holly
bears the crown.*

–"The Holly and the Ivy,"
traditional English carol

FRIDAY 19

NEW MOON

SATURDAY 20

U.S. Space Force Birthday

While in orbit, space shuttles traveled at a maximum speed of about 17,500 mph.

SUNDAY 21

Winter Solstice

Recipes calling for a "knob" of ginger typically mean a 2-inch-long piece.

REMINDERS

DECEMBER						
S	M	T	W	T	F	S
	1	2	3	4	5	6
7	8	9	10	11	12	13
14	15	16	17	18	19	20
21	22	23	24	25	26	27
28	29	30	31			

Complement this planner with daily weather and Almanac wit and wisdom at Almanac.com.

December

22 MONDAY

A fair day in winter is the
mother of a storm.
–English proverb

23 TUESDAY

The names of the
pigs in Walt Disney's
1933 animated short
film *Three Little Pigs*
are Fifer, Fiddler,
and Practical.

24 WEDNESDAY

On this day in 1906,
"O Holy Night" was
played during
the world's first
radio broadcast.

25 THURSDAY

Christmas Day

El Niño, a warm
Pacific Ocean current
that sometimes
appears off South
America around
Christmas, means
"the little boy" in
Spanish, referring to
the Christ Child.

Boxing Day (Canada)

First day of Kwanzaa

During Kwanzaa's
7-day celebration,
a candle is lit each
evening before one
of the holiday's
seven principles
is discussed.

FIRST QUARTER

*Winter is the time for
comfort, for good food
and warmth, for the
touch of a friendly
hand, and for a talk
beside the fire: It is the
time for home.*

–Edith Sitwell, English poet
(1887–1964)

REMINDERS

DECEMBER

S	M	T	W	T	F	S
	1	2	3	4	5	6
7	8	9	10	11	12	13
14	15	16	17	18	19	20
21	22	23	24	25	26	27
28	29	30	31			

Complement this planner with daily weather and Almanac wit and wisdom at Almanac.com.

29 MONDAY

On this day in 1930, Fred Newton became the first person to have swum the length of the Mississippi River.

30 TUESDAY

Toss your natural Christmas tree into the woods to serve as shelter for birds.

31 WEDNESDAY

New Year's Eve

May you have warm words on a cold evening, a full Moon on a dark night, and the road downhill all the way to your door.
–Irish blessing

1 THURSDAY

New Year's Day

January 1 is the official birthday of all Thoroughbred horses in the Northern Hemisphere.

Tomorrow is often the
busiest day of the week.
   –Spanish proverb

FRIDAY 2

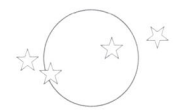

FULL WOLF MOON

SATURDAY 3

The human brain
contains 100,000
miles of blood vessels.

SUNDAY 4

REMINDERS

JANUARY 2026

S	M	T	W	T	F	S
				1	2	3
4	5	6	7	8	9	10
11	12	13	14	15	16	17
18	19	20	21	22	23	24
25	26	27	28	29	30	31

Complement this planner with daily weather and Almanac wit and wisdom at Almanac.com.

bold = *U.S. and/or Canadian national holidays*

JANUARY

S	M	T	W	T	F	S
				1	2	3
4	5	6	7	8	9	10
11	12	13	14	15	16	17
18	**19**	20	21	22	23	24
25	26	27	28	29	30	31

FEBRUARY

S	M	T	W	T	F	S
1	2	3	4	5	6	7
8	9	10	11	12	13	14
15	**16**	17	18	19	20	21
22	23	24	25	26	27	28

MARCH

S	M	T	W	T	F	S
1	2	3	4	5	6	7
8	9	10	11	12	13	14
15	16	17	18	19	20	21
22	23	24	25	26	27	28
29	30	31				

APRIL

S	M	T	W	T	F	S
			1	2	**3**	4
5	**6**	7	8	9	10	11
12	13	14	15	16	17	18
19	20	21	22	23	24	25
26	27	28	29	30		

MAY

S	M	T	W	T	F	S
					1	2
3	4	5	6	7	8	9
10	11	12	13	14	15	16
17	**18**	19	20	21	22	23
24	**25**	26	27	28	29	30
31						

JUNE

S	M	T	W	T	F	S
	1	2	3	4	5	6
7	8	9	10	11	12	13
14	15	16	17	18	**19**	20
21	22	23	24	25	26	27
28	29	30				

JULY

S	M	T	W	T	F	S
		1	2	3	**4**	
5	6	7	8	9	10	11
12	13	14	15	16	17	18
19	20	21	22	23	24	25
26	27	28	29	30	31	

AUGUST

S	M	T	W	T	F	S
						1
2	3	4	5	6	7	8
9	10	11	12	13	14	15
16	17	18	19	20	21	22
23	24	25	26	27	28	29
30	31					

SEPTEMBER

S	M	T	W	T	F	S
		1	2	3	4	5
6	**7**	8	9	10	11	12
13	14	15	16	17	18	19
20	21	22	23	24	25	26
27	28	29	**30**			

OCTOBER

S	M	T	W	T	F	S
				1	2	3
4	5	6	7	8	9	10
11	**12**	13	14	15	16	17
18	19	20	21	22	23	24
25	26	27	28	29	30	31

NOVEMBER

S	M	T	W	T	F	S
1	2	3	4	5	6	7
8	9	10	**11**	12	13	14
15	16	17	18	19	20	21
22	23	24	25	**26**	27	28
29	30					

DECEMBER

S	M	T	W	T	F	S
		1	2	3	4	5
6	7	8	9	10	11	12
13	14	15	16	17	18	19
20	21	22	23	24	**25**	**26**
27	28	29	30	31		

Planning a trip? See the Long-Range Weather Forecast at Almanac.com/Weather.

Passwords

WEB SITE	USER NAME	PASSWORD

Addresses

Name _____ Home _____

Address _____ Work _____

_____ Cell _____

Email _____ Fax _____

Name _____ Home _____

Address _____ Work _____

_____ Cell _____

Email _____ Fax _____

Name _____ Home _____

Address _____ Work _____

_____ Cell _____

Email _____ Fax _____

Name _____ Home _____

Address _____ Work _____

_____ Cell _____

Email _____ Fax _____

Name _____ Home _____

Address _____ Work _____

_____ Cell _____

Email _____ Fax _____

Name _____ Home _____

Address _____ Work _____

_____ Cell _____

Email _____ Fax _____

Name _____ Home _____

Address _____ Work _____

_____ Cell _____

Email _____ Fax _____

Complement this planner with daily weather and Almanac wit and wisdom at Almanac.com.

Important Contacts

In case of emergency, notify:

Name	Home
Address	Work
	Cell
Relationship	Email
Police department	Gas/oil company
Fire department	Electric company
Ambulance	Electrician
Hospital	Plumber
Physician	School(s)
Dentist	Day care
Pharmacy	Baby-sitter
Poison control	Veterinarian
Clergy	Insurance, auto
City/town office	Homeowner's
Carpenter	Health
Auto mechanic	Dental
Cell provider	Credit card(s)
Landline provider	
Internet provider	Bank(s)
Cable/satellite company	
Other	

THE OLD FARMER'S ALMANAC

For gardening advice, weather forecasts, and more, visit **Almanac.com.**

Thank you for choosing this planner. We hope that you enjoy it!

Follow us on social media for more fun every day.